April

Julie Murray

Abdo
MONTHS
Kids

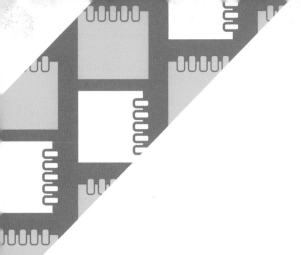

abdopublishing.com

Published by Abdo Kids, a division of ABDO, PO Box 398166, Minneapolis, Minnesota 55439.
Copyright © 2018 by Abdo Consulting Group, Inc. International copyrights reserved in all countries.
No part of this book may be reproduced in any form without written permission from the publisher.

Printed in the United States of America, North Mankato, Minnesota.

052017

092017

Photo Credits: iStock, Shutterstock, ©Brandon Dilbeck p.22 / CC-BY-SA-2.0

Production Contributors: Teddy Borth, Jennie Forsberg, Grace Hansen

Design Contributors: Christina Doffing, Candice Keimig, Dorothy Toth

Publisher's Cataloging in Publication Data

Names: Murray, Julie, 1969-, author.

Title: April / by Julie Murray.

Description: Minneapolis, Minnesota : Abdo Kids, 2018 | Series: Months |
    Includes bibliographical references and index.

Identifiers: LCCN 2016962336 | ISBN 9781532100185 (lib. bdg.) |
    ISBN 9781532100871 (ebook) | ISBN 9781532101427 (Read-to-me ebook)

Subjects: LCSH: April (Month)--Juvenile literature. | Calendar--Juvenile literature.

Classification: DDC 398/.33--dc23

LC record available at http://lccn.loc.gov/2016962336

Table of Contents

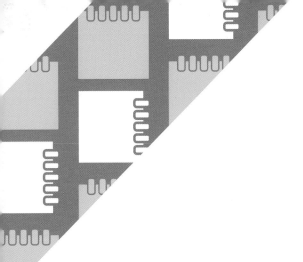

April

There are 12 months
in the year.

January

February

March

April

May

June

July

August

September

October

November

December

5

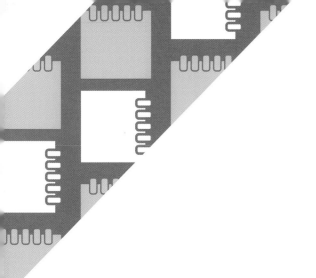

April is the 4th month.

It has 30 days.

April

1	2	3	4	5	6	7
8	9	10	11	12	13	14
15	16	17	18	19	20	21
22	23	24	25	26	27	28
29	30					

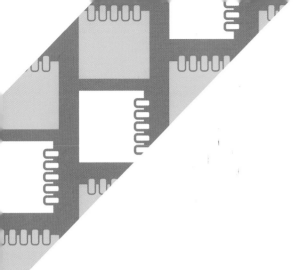

April Fool's Day is on the 1st.

Ana plays a joke on Dan.

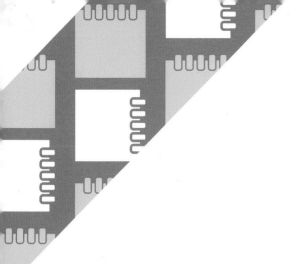

Thomas Jefferson was born on April 13th. He was the third US president.

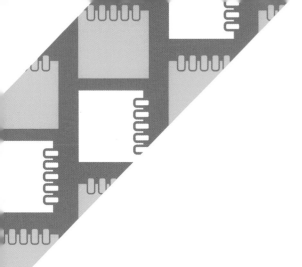

The 22nd is Earth Day!

Ben picks up litter.

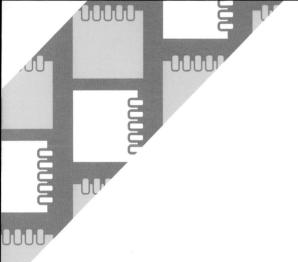

Arbor Day is in April. It is on the last Friday. Joe plants a tree!

14

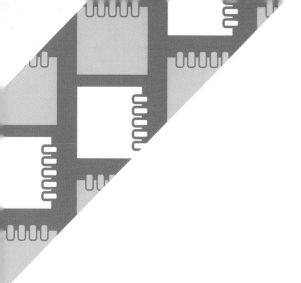

Easter is often in April.

So is Passover.

16

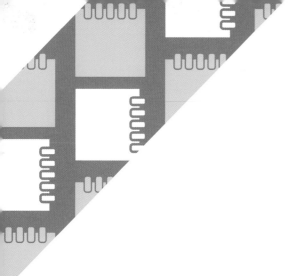

It can rain in April. Eva puts on her red boots.

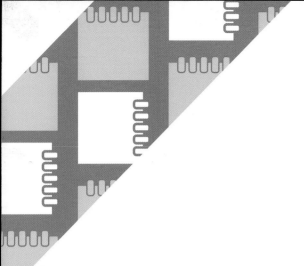

Abe plays in the rain.

He loves April!

Fun Days in April

Grilled Cheese Sandwich Day
April 12

Jackie Robinson Day
April 15

National Jelly Bean Day
April 22

National Pretzel Day
April 26

Glossary

Arbor Day
a day dedicated to planting trees.

Easter
a Christian holiday that celebrates Jesus Christ rising from the dead.

litter
trash, like paper, cans, and bottles, that is left lying in a public place.

Passover
a Jewish holiday that celebrates the Hebrews being freed from slavery.

Index

abdokids.com

Use this code to log on to abdokids.com and access crafts, games, videos, and more!

Abdo Kids Code:
MAK0185